Hooray for Dairy Farming!

A Bobbie Kalman Book
Crabtree Publishing Company

Hooray for Dairy Farming!
A Bobbie Kalman Book

For Irene Larin and Michel Baril

Editor-in-Chief
Bobbie Kalman

Writing team
Bobbie Kalman
Allison Larin
Niki Walker

Managing editor
Lynda Hale

Text and photo research
Allison Larin

Editors
Niki Walker
Greg Nickles

Computer design
Lynda Hale

Cover design
Lynda Hale
Campbell Creative Services

Production coordinator
Hannelore Sotzek

Teacher Consultants from
Ontario Agri-Food Education

Special thanks to
Mike Baril; James McDonald; Karen Mantel, Bill Mitchell, and
Jim Fitzgerald of Dairy Farmers of Ontario; Robert J. Huffman/
Field Mark Publications; Victoria Village Public School; and
Sandra Hawkins of Ontario Agri-Food Education

Photographs
AGstockUSA: Larry Fleming: pages 28, 29; Mark Gibson: page 21 (bottom);
   David Halsey: pages 15 (top), 18; Holly Kuper: page 15 (bottom);
   Rick Mooney: pages 14, 25; Russ Munn: page 10; Thomas Schneider:
   page 12; Fredrick Schussler: page 4; Lynn Stone: title page, page 26
Alinari/Art Resource, NY: page 6
William H. Allen, Jr.: page 13 (top)
Marc Crabtree: page 31 (bottom)
Erich Lessing/Art Resource, NY: page 7
Renee Lynn/Photo Researchers, Inc.: front cover (detail)
Jerry Howard/Positive Images: page 16
Tom Stack & Associates: Bob Pool: page 21 (top left);
   Inga Spence: pages 5, 13 (bottom), 23 (both)
Joseph Stanski/Morning Star Photo: page 17
Jerry Whitaker: page 21 (top right)

Illustrations
Barbara Bedell: border on all pages, page 7
Cori Marvin: pages 8-9, 10, 11, 19, 22, 27

CADCC

Crabtree Publishing Company

350 Fifth Avenue
Suite 3308
New York
N.Y. 10118

360 York Road, RR 4,
Niagara-on-the-Lake,
Ontario, Canada
L0S 1J0

73 Lime Walk
Headington
Oxford OX3 7AD
United Kingdom

ME

Cataloging in Publication Data
Bobbie Kalman
   Hooray for dairy farming!

(Hooray for farming!)
Includes index.

ISBN 0-86505-650-1 (library bound)   ISBN 0-86505-664-1 (pbk.)
This book looks at life on a dairy farm, describing how the cows are
housed, fed, cared for, and milked.

1. Dairy farming—Juvenile literature. 2. Cows—Juvenile literature.
3. Dairy cattle—Juvenile literature. [1. Dairy farming. 2. Cows.]
I. Title. II. Series: Kalman, Bobbie. Hooray for farming!

SF239.5.K35 1997   j636.2'142   LC 97-39876
                                                CIP

Milk from moo to you!

What is dairy farming?	4
Dairy farms in the past	6
At the dairy farm	8
The dairy barn	10
The herd	12
Calves	14
I am bull. Hear me roar!	16
How do cows make milk?	19
Milking time!	20
Moo-ving milk to a dairy	22
Feeding and cleaning	24
Healthy cows are happy cows	27
Calving	28
Milk is nutritious!	30
Dairy farming words & Index	32

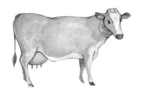

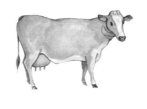
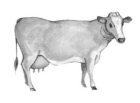

Dairy farms in the past

People began dairy farming over 5,000 years ago, but they did not drink much milk because it could make them sick. Most milk was made into cheese and butter.

Natural **bacteria** live in milk. Bacteria are tiny creatures that can make people sick. Bacteria also make milk turn sour.

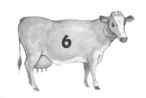

6

Pioneers and cows

Before the 1700s there were no cows in North America. Pioneers brought cows with them from other countries. Many families had only one cow. It was called a **house cow**. The house cow made just enough milk for the family. The family had to use the milk right away because people did not have a refrigerator to keep food from going bad.

Making milk safe to drink

In the 1800s, a man named Louis Pasteur, shown left, found a way to get rid of bacteria in milk. He heated milk quickly to a very high temperature. The heat killed enough of the bacteria that people could drink milk without getting sick. This process was named after him. It is called **pasteurization**.

Milk can also be kept longer if it is refrigerated. Bacteria grow easily in warm liquids. Bacteria cannot grow as quickly in cold liquid.

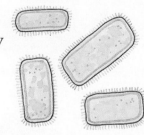

bacteria

At the dairy farm

A dairy farm is a very busy place.
It has different areas where the cows
are fed, milked, and looked after.

silo

milk truck

milking parlor

8

Cows spend most of the winter in the barn. In summer, they go inside only at night and when they go to the **milking parlor**.

The **silo** is where food called **silage** is made and kept. Farmers put corn in the silo and, over time, it becomes silage. It is mixed with hay and fed to the cows in winter.

Cows spend a lot of time in the **pasture**. This field has grasses and other plants that the cows eat. A fence stops the cows from wandering away.

During winter, the cows get fresh air and exercise in the **barnyard**, a fenced area close to the barn.

pasture

barnyard

9

The dairy barn

The barn is where almost all the work is done on a dairy farm. Cows sleep, eat, and are cleaned and milked in the barn. There are three different types of dairy barns: **free-stall barns**, **tie-stall barns**, and **open-air corrals**.

Free-stall barns

Free-stall barns are the most common type of dairy barn. They are used on large dairy farms. They have rows of open stalls where the cows sleep. A **feed alley** runs down the middle of the barn, between stalls. Tractors drive down the feed alley and drop food into it.

stall

feed alley

10

Tie-stall

Tie-stall barns are used on small dairy farms. There is one stall for each cow. A cow spends most of its time in its stall. It can move around enough to eat and sleep. A rope or chain keeps the cow from getting out. The cows are not taken out of their stall to be milked. The farmer brings the milking machines to the cows.

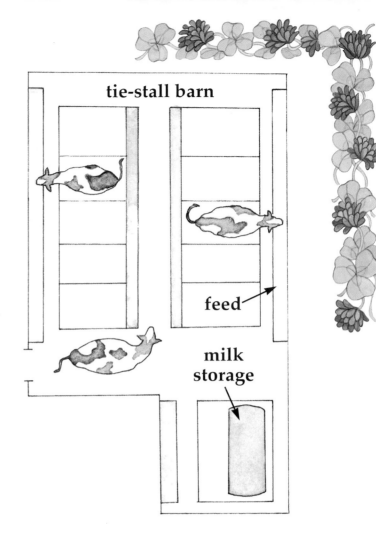

tie-stall barn

feed

milk storage

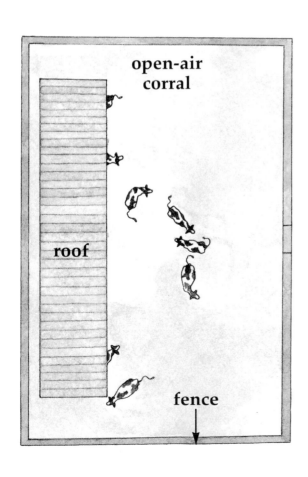

open-air corral

roof

fence

Open-air corral

In warm places, dairy farmers use open-air corrals. The cows are kept inside a **corral**, or fenced-in area, where they can walk around, eat grass, or lie down. There is a roof over part of the corral. The cows stand underneath it when it rains or when the sun gets too hot.

11

The herd

A group of many cows is called a **herd**.
A small herd has about ten cows. A large
herd can have hundreds. Male cows are
called **bulls**. Most herds have one bull and
many females. Only females can make milk.
They make it to feed their babies, which are
called **calves**. Cows make more milk than
their calves need. Dairy farmers collect this
extra milk and sell it.

12

When is a cow a cow?

Most people simply call all types of cows "cows." Farmers, however, have different names for male and female cows of different ages. A young cow is called a calf until it is about nine months old. A male (shown right) is then called a bull, and a female is called a **heifer**. After a heifer has her first calf, she is called a cow.

Which cow is which?

To tell their cows apart, many farmers put ear tags on each one. The tag has a number on it, and the cows are known by this number. Some farmers put a chain necklace with a numbered tag around the neck of every cow.

Calves

When it is time for a pregnant cow to have her calf, the farmer takes her into the barn. A cow usually has only one calf at a time. Sometimes a cow gives birth to twins.

Calves are much smaller than adult cows. At first a calf is weak and cannot stand up, but it quickly grows strong. It can walk an hour after it is born. The farmer then weighs the calf and checks it to make sure it is healthy.

A calf's first meal

Sometimes farmers have to help a calf find its mother's **udder**, which is where milk comes out. They make sure that the calf gets its mother's **colostrum**.

Colostrum is the first milk that a cow makes for her calf. It is yellow and more nutritious than regular milk. Colostrum helps the calf grow big and strong faster. It also helps calves fight off diseases.

Meeting the herd

A new calf is ready to join the herd a few days after it is born. The calf knows which cow is its mother, and it goes to her for food and comfort. The calf is **weaned** when it is about six weeks old. It stops drinking its mother's milk and learns to eat solid foods such as grass.

I am bull. Hear me roar!

Bulls are larger and stronger than cows.
Many have sharp horns and short tempers.
Most dairy farmers keep only one bull. It is
usually kept apart from the rest of the herd.

Nasty but necessary

Bulls eat a lot of food and do not make any milk. They are very expensive to keep, but they are needed on a dairy farm. A bull **mates** with the cows so that they will have calves. The cows make milk for the calves and the dairy farmer sells some of this milk.

A nose ring

Farmers treat their bull with great care. They do not want to make the bull angry. One way to control a bull is to put a ring through its nose. The dairy farmer ties up the bull by its nose ring. The bull does not pull on the rope or chain because doing so hurts its nose.

How do cows make milk?

Cows eat a lot of food each day. Their body uses almost half of this food to make milk. A cow's milk tastes a little like the food it eats. If a cow eats clover, for example, its milk will taste sweet because clover is sweet. Most farmers make sure their cows eat sweet grasses so that their milk will taste good.

clover

Udderly fantastic!

Cows make milk in their udder. The udder is a pouch divided into four separate parts. Inside the udder are **lumens**, which make tiny drops of milk. When the lumens fill up with milk, the milk passes through tiny tubes to the **teats**. Each part of the udder has a teat. Milk comes out of a teat when the cow is milked or when she feeds her baby.

teats

udder

Milking time!

A cow must be milked two or three times every day. Cows feel much better after their udders are emptied. Udders that are too full get sore.

Modern milking

People used to milk cows by hand, two teats at a time. Today, milking machines milk cows much faster than people ever could by hand.

Milking machines

A milking machine has four cups connected to a tube. Each cup fits over a teat and gently sucks out the milk. When the milk stops flowing, the cup automatically stops sucking.

Where does the milk go?

The milk moves through a tube in the milking machine and flows to a storage room in the barn. In this storage room, milk is kept in a refrigerated tank. The milk is cooled in the tank so that bacteria will not turn it sour.

20

Milking by hand.

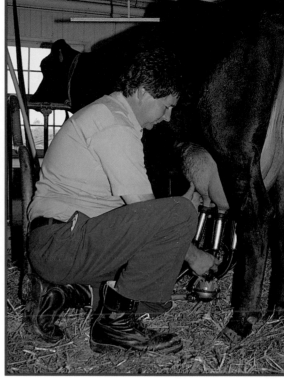

Milking with a machine.

The milking parlor

Before a cow is milked, its udders and teats are cleaned so that no dirt or germs will get into the milk. In a milking parlor, the cows are put into raised stalls. The people working the milking machines stand below the cows. From below, the cows' udders are easier to reach. People do not have to bend down to attach the milking machines to the cows' teats.

Cows eat a lot of food, and they make a lot of milk. One cow makes about 100 glasses of it a day! The **raw milk**, taken from the cows, is kept in a storage tank. A big milk truck comes to the farm every two days to pick up the raw milk. The milk is pumped into the truck's refrigerated tank, which keeps it cold during the trip to the **dairy**.

At the dairy

A dairy is a factory where milk is put into jugs, cartons, and bags, or is used to make other foods. When the milk reaches the dairy, it is pasteurized in a big tank. It is no longer raw. Some of the milk is then packaged and sent to stores, where it is sold. The rest is used to make dairy products such as cheese, sour cream, yogurt, whipped cream, and ice cream.

(above) Some milk is used for making cheese. To make cheese, milk is left in a big vat so that it goes sour and separates into **curds** and **whey**. Whey is the liquid, and curds are the fresh cheese. The worker in the picture above is blending the milk with a rake, which speeds up the cheese making.

(right) It takes a whole lot of milk to make this round of cheese.

Feeding and cleaning

There are many chores that must be done on a dairy farm. Besides milking the cows, the dairy farmer must feed them, keep them clean, and tidy the barn.

Dairy farmers feed their cows two or three times a day. They mix corn silage, hay, and vitamins for the cows to eat while they are being milked. This mixture of food gives the cows extra nutrients that they do not get from the grass in the pasture. Cows need a lot of nutrients to make good milk!

Hay time

Late July and early August is hay time on dairy farms. Hay is long grasses such as clover or alfalfa that have been cut and dried to use as animal food. Farmers cut the grass with a big mower and leave it to dry in the field for about two days. The dry hay is bundled into round **bales** and stored in the barn.

24

Clean cows

Clean cows give clean milk. Cows are also healthier when they are kept clean. The farmer washes the cows when they get dirty in the barnyard or pasture and cleans out their stalls every day. The dirty straw is taken out, and the stalls are sprayed with soapy water.

Healthy cows are happy cows

It is important for a dairy farm to have healthy, happy cows. Sick cows do not make good milk. Sometimes they do not make any milk at all. Dairy farmers keep their cows clean to prevent diseases. They also keep a close eye on the cows to make sure they are not injured.

Dairy farmers inspect their cows often to find injuries or illnesses. They check the eyes for infection and examine the body closely for any cuts or sores. The farmer also looks for any bugs that live on the cows. Bugs bother cows and sometimes make them sick.

Trim those hoofs!

Cow hoofs are like people's fingernails—they are always growing. When a cow's hoofs get too long, the cow cannot walk properly. The dairy farmer trims the hoofs once or twice a year so that the cows' feet will not get sore. The farmer uses a sharp knife or clippers for trimming the hoofs.

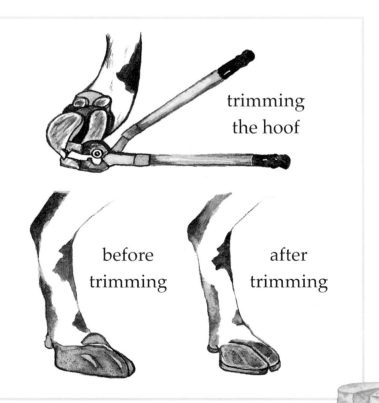

trimming the hoof

before trimming

after trimming

27

Calving

Dairy farmers sell milk from their cows to earn a living. Cows make milk to feed their calves, so farmers make sure that all their cows get pregnant every year. New calves also replace older cows that get sick or die.

A heifer has her first calf when she is two years old. She is pregnant for nine months before giving birth. Cows give birth to their calves in early spring. The period of time during which cows are pregnant, give birth, and care for their calves is called **calving**.

The calving pen

Cows give birth in a **calving pen**, shown above. A calving pen is a small, separated area of the barn. The pen stops other cows from bothering the mother while she gives birth. There is enough room in the pen for the cow to lie down and for the farmer to help her or the calf. The pen is kept even cleaner than the rest of the barn so that the mother and her calf will not become ill from dirt and germs.

Milk is nutritious!

Milk is delicious and nutritious. It is almost all water, but it is packed with many nutrients. Milk is a major source of protein, which people need to stay alive and grow. Milk is also rich in minerals such as calcium and magnesium, which help form strong bones and teeth.

The minerals in milk help make strong bones and muscles. Milk also has vitamins such as vitamin D, which help your bones.

The vitamins in milk help repair the tissues in your body. Vitamins also give you plenty of energy for playing hard!

Milk helps your eyes stay healthy so you can see well both day and night.

Milk makes your brain strong, too, so you can use it to learn all kinds of new things.

Make a banana milkshake!

You will need:

1 cup milk
1 banana
1 scoop vanilla or chocolate ice cream

Put all the ingredients into a blender. Blend on high speed for 30 seconds, or until mixture is smooth. Pour the shake into a tall glass and enjoy! For a different taste, try strawberries, peaches, or raspberries instead of the banana.

Dairy farming words

bacteria Tiny living things that can be seen only through a microscope

bull A male cow

calf A young bull or cow

graze To feed on growing grass

herd A group of plant-eating animals

mate To make babies

nutrient A substance that the body needs to stay healthy

pasteurization The process of heating raw milk to a high temperature and cooling it quickly in order to kill bacteria

pasture A large fenced field where grasses and other small plants grow

raw milk Milk that is not yet pasteurized

silage Livestock food that has been stored in a silo to ferment

silo A tower used for storing animal food

teat A small projection on an udder out of which milk comes

udder A large pouch on the underside of a cow that makes milk

wean To make a baby used to eating food other than its mother's milk

Index

bacteria 6, 7, 20

barns 5, 9, 10-11, 14, 20, 24, 29

barnyard 9, 25

body 13, 16, 17, 19, 27

bulls 12, 13, 16-17

calves 5, 12, 13, 14-15, 17, 19, 28-29

chores 5, 8, 10, 24-25, 29

cows, types of 7, 12-13

dairy 22

dairy products 4, 5, 6, 12, 22, 30-31

eating 5, 8, 9, 10, 11, 15, 17, 19, 22, 24

farmers 4, 5, 9, 11, 12, 13, 14, 15, 16, 17, 19, 24, 25, 27, 28, 29

farms 8-9, 10, 11, 17, 22, 24, 27

food 7, 9, 11, 15, 17, 19, 22, 24

grazing 5

health 14, 15, 25, 27, 28, 29

heifer 13, 28

herd 12-13, 15, 16

milking 5, 19, 20-21, 24

milking machines 20, 21

milking parlor 8, 9, 21

milk products *see* dairy products

milk truck 8, 22-23

Pasteur, Louis 7

pasteurization 7, 22

pasture 9, 24, 25

recipe 31

refrigeration 7, 20, 22

teats 19, 20, 21

udder 15, 19, 20, 21

32

1 2 3 4 5 6 7 8 9 0 Printed in the U.S.A. 6 5 4 3 2 1 0 9 8 7